"Unlocking the Power of AI Prompts: A Beginner's Guide"

-BY Amit Gupta

Disclaimer

This book is intended to provide an introduction to AI prompt engineering for beginners and is not a substitute for professional advice. The information contained in this book is provided "as is" and without warranty of any kind, express or implied. The author and publisher of this book make no representation or warranty, including but not limited to, the accuracy, suitability, or completeness of the information in this book. The author and publisher will not be liable for any direct, indirect, incidental, consequential, or special damages arising out of or in any way connected with the use of this book or the information contained herein. Always consult a qualified professional before making any decisions based on the information in this book.

TABLE OF CONTENT

Chapter 7: Challenges and Limitations of AI Prompt Engineering

Ethical considerations when using AI prompts

Legal and ethical implications of using AI-generated content in different contexts

Limitations of current AI technology and potential pitfalls to avoid

Strategies for overcoming common challenges in AI prompt engineering

Future directions for AI prompt engineering

Chapter 8: Conclusion and Next Steps

Recap of key takeaways from the book

Resources for further learning and practice

Examples of innovative uses of AI prompts in different industries

Final thoughts on the importance of AI prompt engineering

Final thoughts on the importance of AI prompt engineering

The importance of ongoing learning and experimentation in AI prompt engineering

Future directions for AI prompt engineering and the role of beginners in shaping the field.

9. Career options for AI Prompt Engineer

Job options for AI Prompt Engineer

Freelancing and business options for AI Prompt Engineer

1. Introduction to AI Prompt Engineering

Welcome to the world of AI Prompt Engineering! In this book, we'll be diving into the exciting field of artificial intelligence (AI) and exploring how prompts can be used to create more efficient and effective AI systems.

So what is AI prompt engineering, exactly? Simply put, it's the process of designing prompts that instruct AI systems on what actions to take or what information to provide. This can include everything from generating personalized content to analyzing large datasets.

Throughout this book, we'll be exploring the various approaches to AI prompt engineering and discussing real-world applications of the technology. We'll also be covering the fundamentals of AI language models and natural language processing (NLP), as well as advanced techniques for optimizing AI prompts and handling out-of-domain topics.

Whether you're a beginner looking to learn more about AI prompt engineering or an experienced practitioner seeking to refine your skills, this book has something for you. So let's dive in and explore the exciting world of AI prompt engineering together!

What is AI prompt engineering?

AI prompt engineering is a process of developing artificial intelligence models by using natural language processing (NLP) techniques to generate high-quality text prompts. In other words, AI prompt engineering involves creating prompts or starting points for machine learning models to generate responses or output.

For example, imagine you want to create an AI chatbot that can answer customer queries. Instead of manually coding responses for every possible customer query, you can use AI prompt engineering to create a set of prompts that the chatbot can use to generate responses. These prompts can be created using NLP techniques to ensure that they are effective in generating high-quality responses.

To better understand this concept, readers can try exercises like creating prompts for a chatbot to answer common questions about a particular topic. For instance, they could create prompts for a chatbot to answer questions about a popular movie, book or game. By doing this, readers will understand how AI prompt engineering can simplify the development of AI models and make them more effective.

Real-world applications of AI prompt engineering

AI prompt engineering has numerous real-world applications, and its use is becoming increasingly common in various industries. Here are some examples of how AI prompt engineering is being used:

Chatbots and virtual assistants: AI prompt engineering is used to develop chatbots and virtual assistants that can interact with users and answer their questions. By creating effective prompts, these chatbots can generate more accurate and helpful responses.

Content creation: AI prompt engineering can be used to generate prompts for content creation. For example, AI models can be used to generate article titles or social media post ideas.

Creative writing: AI prompt engineering can be used to assist writers in generating ideas for stories or creative writing. By providing effective prompts, AI can help writers overcome writer's block and develop more interesting storylines.

Language translation: AI prompt engineering is used in machine translation to generate prompts for translations. These prompts can help the AI generate more accurate translations and reduce the amount of human input required.

To help readers understand how AI prompt engineering is being used in the real world, they can try exercises like creating prompts for a chatbot or virtual assistant, generating article titles using AI models, or developing story ideas using prompts generated by AI. By doing these exercises, readers will better understand the practical applications of AI prompt engineering.

Different approaches to AI prompt engineering

There are different approaches to AI prompt engineering, and each approach has its advantages and disadvantages. Here are some of the most common approaches to AI prompt engineering:

Rule-based approach: This approach involves using a set of pre-defined rules to generate prompts. For example, a rule-based approach can be used to generate prompts for a chatbot. However, this approach can be limited in its flexibility and may not be able to handle complex prompts.

Statistical approach: This approach involves using statistical models to generate prompts. For example, statistical models can be used to generate article titles or social media post ideas. However, this approach may not always produce the most creative or interesting prompts.

Machine learning approach: This approach involves using machine learning algorithms to learn from data and generate prompts. For example, a machine learning approach can be used to generate story ideas or assist writers in developing more interesting storylines. This approach can be more flexible than rule-based or statistical approaches and can produce more creative prompts.

To help readers understand the different approaches to AI prompt engineering, they can try exercises like developing rule-based prompts for a chatbot, generating statistical prompts for social media posts, or using machine learning algorithms to generate prompts for creative writing. By doing these exercises, readers will better understand the advantages and disadvantages of each approach and be able to choose the best approach for their needs.

Why is it important for beginners to learn AI prompt engineering?

It is important for beginners to learn AI prompt engineering because it is a rapidly growing field with a wide range of applications. With the increasing use of AI in various industries, there is a growing demand for professionals who have expertise in AI prompt engineering.

Furthermore, AI prompt engineering has the potential to improve and enhance existing technologies, leading to greater efficiency and accuracy. It also allows for the development of new and innovative solutions to complex problems.

Learning AI prompt engineering can provide a competitive edge in their future career paths. It can also stimulate their curiosity and creativity by encouraging them to explore new possibilities and experiment with different approaches.

Overall, understanding AI prompt engineering is becoming increasingly important in today's technological world, and having knowledge in this field can lead to numerous opportunities for personal and professional growth.

2: Understanding AI Language Models

What are AI language models?

AI language models are a type of artificial intelligence that has been trained to understand and generate human language. These models are designed to analyze and learn from large amounts of data, and then use that knowledge to generate new language that sounds natural and fluent. In other words, an AI language model can be thought of as a virtual language user that is capable of processing and producing language just like a human.

Examples of AI language models include GPT-3, BERT, and OpenAI Codex. These models have become increasingly popular in recent years, as they have the potential to revolutionize a wide range of industries, from healthcare and finance to marketing and entertainment. However, understanding how AI language models work and their limitations is crucial for beginners to get started in AI prompt engineering.

How do they work?

AI language models are designed to learn the patterns and structure of language through a process called natural language processing (NLP). These models use large amounts of text data to identify patterns and relationships in the language, and then use these patterns to generate new text that appears to be written by a human.

The basic working principle of an AI language model is to take a sequence of words as input and then use the patterns learned from the training data to predict the next word in the sequence. The model repeats this process to generate a complete sentence or paragraph.

For example, let's say we have a simple AI language model that has been trained on a large corpus of text about cats. We can give the model the input "The black cat sat on the" and ask it to generate the next word. Based on the patterns it has learned, the model may predict "windowsill" as the next word, resulting in the output "The black cat sat on the windowsill."

To further illustrate this process, we can provide exercises to the readers to try generating their own text using a pre-trained language model such as GPT-3. For instance, we can ask the readers to provide a starting sentence or phrase, and then ask them to use GPT-3 to generate a new paragraph or story based on that prompt. This will help the readers to better understand how AI language models work in practice.

Differences between popular AI language models such as GPT-3, BERT, and OpenAI Codex

GPT-3, BERT, and OpenAI Codex are some of the most popular AI language models. Each of these models uses a different architecture and approach to process and understand human language. In this answer, we'll explore the key differences between these models.

GPT-3 (Generative Pre-trained Transformer 3):

GPT-3 is a generative language model that uses unsupervised learning to generate human-like text. It was trained on a massive corpus of text data and can be used for a wide range of language tasks, such as language translation, chatbots, and content generation. GPT-3 is capable of generating human-like text with high accuracy and can even complete tasks that it has not been specifically trained on.

Example:
"Prompt: Write an article about the benefits of exercise.
GPT-3 generated response: Exercise is a crucial part of a healthy lifestyle. Regular exercise can help you lose weight, reduce your risk of chronic diseases, and improve your mental health. Whether you prefer running, yoga, or weightlifting, there is an exercise that can benefit you."

BERT (Bidirectional Encoder Representations from Transformers):

BERT is a language model that uses a bidirectional transformer to process text in both directions. It can be fine-tuned for a variety of natural language processing tasks, such as text classification, question answering, and named entity recognition. BERT is particularly effective at understanding the context of a sentence and can be used to generate highly accurate language models.

Example:
"Prompt: What is the capital of France?
BERT generated response: The capital of France is Paris."

OpenAI Codex:

OpenAI Codex is an AI model that uses deep learning and natural language processing to understand and generate code. It has been trained on a vast corpus of code and can be used to generate code, suggest fixes, and even answer coding questions. OpenAI Codex is capable of generating code in a variety of programming languages, including Python, JavaScript, and Ruby.

Example:
"Prompt: Write a Python function to calculate the sum of two numbers.
OpenAI Codex generated response:
python

```
Copy code
def sum(a, b): return a + b
```

In conclusion, GPT-3, BERT, and OpenAI Codex are all powerful language models that can be used for a variety of natural language processing tasks. GPT-3 is primarily used for content generation, while BERT is used for text classification and question answering. OpenAI Codex is unique in that it can generate code and answer coding questions. Each of these models has its strengths and weaknesses, and the choice of model depends on the specific use case."

The impact of training data and biases on AI language models

Training data and biases are critical factors that can significantly impact the performance and fairness of AI language models. In this answer, we will explore how training data and biases can impact AI language models and the ways in which these issues can be addressed.

Training data:

The quality and quantity of training data can have a significant impact on the performance of AI language models. AI language models like GPT-3 and BERT are typically trained on large datasets of text, and the quality of these datasets can impact the accuracy and effectiveness of the resulting model.

For example, if a language model is trained on a dataset that contains a limited range of language structures or vocabulary, it may struggle to generate or understand text that is outside of this limited range. Similarly, if a dataset contains biased or inappropriate content, the resulting language model may replicate this bias in its generated text.

Biases:

AI language models can also be biased in their outputs, reflecting the biases present in the data they were trained on. This can manifest in a variety of ways, such as gender or racial bias in language generation or discrimination in natural language processing tasks.

For example, a language model trained on a dataset that contains predominantly male-authored texts may struggle to generate text from a female perspective or use gender-neutral language. Similarly, a natural language processing model that was trained on a biased dataset may discriminate against certain groups in its processing of language.

The impact of training data and biases on AI language models

Addressing biases in AI language models and training data:

To address these issues, it is crucial to consider the quality and diversity of the training data used to train AI language models. Data sets must be carefully curated to ensure that they are representative of the language being modeled, and measures must be taken to mitigate the impact of biases that may be present in the data.

One approach to addressing biases is to incorporate fairness and diversity metrics into the training process to identify and mitigate potential biases. Additionally, techniques like data augmentation can be used to generate more diverse training data and reduce bias.

In conclusion, training data and biases are critical factors that can significantly impact the accuracy and fairness of AI language models. By carefully curating training data and implementing techniques to mitigate bias, we can ensure that AI language models are more accurate and fair in their outputs.

How to choose the right AI language model for your needs

Choosing the right AI language model for your needs requires careful consideration of several factors, including the specific use case, the size and quality of the available training data, and the required level of accuracy and performance. In this answer, we'll explore the key factors to consider when choosing an AI language model and provide some examples of popular models that are commonly used for different language tasks.

Consider the specific use case:

Different AI language models are designed for different language tasks. For example, GPT-3 is a powerful language generation model that can be used for a wide range of content generation tasks, while BERT is an effective model for text classification and question answering. It's important to consider the specific language task you're trying to accomplish and choose a model that is optimized for that task.

Consider the size and quality of available training data:

The size and quality of the available training data can also impact the choice of AI language model. Some models, such as GPT-3, require access to massive amounts of training data to perform effectively, while others, such as BERT, can perform well with smaller datasets. It's important to consider the size and quality of the available training data and choose a model that can be effectively trained with that data.

Consider the required level of accuracy and performance:

The required level of accuracy and performance is another critical factor to consider when choosing an AI language model. Some models, such as GPT-3, are known for their high levels of accuracy and can generate human-like text with high fidelity, while others may be more appropriate for tasks where a lower level of accuracy is acceptable.

Example:
Suppose you're working on a project that requires a language model to generate news headlines. You have a large dataset of news articles, and you need a model that can generate headlines that accurately reflect the content of the articles. In this case, a model like GPT-3 or T5, which are specifically designed for content generation tasks, may be a good choice.

On the other hand, suppose you're working on a project that requires a language model to classify emails into different categories based on their content. In this case, a model like BERT, which is optimized for text classification, may be a better choice.

In conclusion, choosing the right AI language model for your needs requires careful consideration of several factors, including the specific use case, the size and quality of the available training data, and the required level of accuracy and performance. By considering these factors and choosing a model that is optimized for your specific use case, you can ensure that your language model is effective and accurate.

3: Fundamentals of Prompt Engineering

What is a prompt?

In the context of AI language models, a prompt is a piece of text that is used to initiate or guide the generation of additional text by the model. The prompt provides a starting point or context for the model's generation, which can help to shape the content and style of the generated text.

Prompts can take a variety of forms, depending on the specific task and model being used. For example, a prompt for a language generation task may be a sentence or phrase that provides a starting point for the model to generate additional text, while a prompt for a text classification task may be a piece of text that needs to be classified into a particular category.

Here are a few examples of prompts for different language tasks:

Language Generation Prompt:

Prompt: "Write a short story about a person who discovers a mysterious object in their backyard."

Text Classification Prompt:

Prompt: "Classify the following sentence as positive, negative, or neutral: 'The new restaurant in town is amazing.'"

Question Answering Prompt:

Prompt: "Answer the following question: What is the capital city of France?"

Prompts can be used to fine-tune the output of AI language models, helping to ensure that the generated text is appropriate and accurate for a given task or context. Additionally, prompts can be combined with other techniques, such as conditioning and sampling, to generate more diverse and nuanced text.

In conclusion, a prompt is a piece of text used to guide the generation of additional text by an AI language model. By providing a starting point or context for the model's generation, prompts can help to shape the content and style of the generated text and improve the accuracy and appropriateness of the model's outputs.

How to design a good prompt

Designing a good prompt is important for ensuring that the output of an AI language model is accurate and appropriate for a given task or context. Here are some key tips for designing effective prompts:

Be specific and clear:

The prompt should be specific and clear about the task or context the model is being asked to perform. This can help to reduce ambiguity and improve the accuracy of the generated text. For example, if the prompt is asking the model to generate a product review, it should be clear which product is being reviewed and what aspects of the product should be discussed.

Use natural language:

The prompt should use natural language that is similar to the type of text the model is being asked to generate. This can help the model better understand the task and generate more accurate and appropriate text. For example, if the model is being asked to generate a news article, the prompt should use language similar to that found in news articles.

Provide relevant context:

The prompt should provide relevant context for the model to generate text that is appropriate and accurate for the task. This can include information such as the topic, audience, tone, or style of the text. For example, if the model is being asked to generate a marketing email, the prompt should provide information about the target audience, the product or service being marketed, and the desired tone or style of the email.

Include examples:

Including examples of the desired output can help the model better understand the task and generate more accurate and appropriate text. For example, if the model is being asked to generate a movie synopsis, the prompt could include a few example synopses to help guide the model's generation.

Test and refine:

Once a prompt has been designed, it's important to test and refine it to ensure that the generated text is accurate and appropriate for the task. This may involve testing the model's outputs with different prompts or making adjustments to the prompt based on feedback from users.

In conclusion, designing a good prompt involves being specific and clear, using natural language, providing relevant context, including examples, and testing and refining the prompt to ensure that the generated text is accurate and appropriate for the task. By following these tips, you can design effective prompts that help AI language models generate high-quality text for a variety of tasks and contexts.

Key elements of a prompt

A prompt is a crucial element in guiding an AI language model to generate relevant and appropriate text for a given task. Here are the key elements that should be included in a prompt:

Task or objective: A prompt should specify the task or objective that the model is being asked to perform. This helps the model to understand the desired output and generate text that is relevant and appropriate for the task. For example, if the task is to generate a product review, the prompt should clearly specify that the model is expected to generate a review of a specific product.

Context: The context of the task should be provided in the prompt to help the model generate text that is appropriate and accurate for the task. This can include information such as the target audience, tone, style, or genre of the text. For example, if the task is to generate a news article, the prompt should provide information about the topic, target audience, and the desired tone and style of the article.

Instructions: Instructions should be provided in the prompt to guide the model on what type of text to generate and what information to include. This can include specific questions to answer, prompts for specific types of content to include, or guidance on the length and format of the text. For example, if the task is to generate a product review, the prompt may provide instructions such as "Include information about the product's features, usability, and value for money."

Examples: Examples of the desired output can be included in the prompt to help the model better understand the task and generate more accurate and appropriate text. This can include examples of similar text, such as previous reviews, news articles, or marketing materials. For example, if the task is to generate a marketing email, the prompt may provide examples of previous successful marketing emails.

Constraints: Constraints may be included in the prompt to limit the type of text generated by the model. This can include limitations on the length of the text, specific vocabulary or terminology to be used, or restrictions on the content of the text. For example, if the task is to generate a legal document, the prompt may include constraints such as the specific legal terminology that must be used and restrictions on the content of the document.

In conclusion, a prompt should include the task or objective, context, instructions, examples, and constraints to guide an AI language model in generating relevant and appropriate text for a given task. By including these key elements in the prompt, the model can better understand the desired output and generate text that meets the requirements of the task.

Overview of natural language processing (NLP) and its role in AI prompt engineering

Natural language processing (NLP) is a subfield of artificial intelligence (AI) that deals with the interaction between human language and computers. NLP involves the development of algorithms and models that can analyze, understand, and generate human language.

In the context of AI prompt engineering, NLP plays a critical role in helping to design effective prompts that guide an AI language model to generate relevant and appropriate text for a given task. NLP techniques can be used to analyze and understand the natural language input provided in a prompt, as well as to generate natural language output from the AI language model.

NLP techniques that are commonly used in AI prompt engineering include:

> **Text preprocessing:** This involves cleaning and transforming raw text input into a format that can be easily analyzed by NLP algorithms. Text preprocessing techniques may include removing punctuation, converting text to lowercase, and tokenizing text into individual words or phrases.

> **Sentiment analysis:** This involves analyzing the sentiment or emotion expressed in a given

piece of text. Sentiment analysis can be used to guide the tone and style of the text generated by an AI language model, depending on the desired emotional response from the target audience.

Named entity recognition: This involves identifying and categorizing named entities, such as people, organizations, and locations, in a given piece of text. Named entity recognition can be used to guide the content of the text generated by an AI language model, depending on the specific entities or topics that need to be included.

Text classification: This involves categorizing a given piece of text into one or more predefined categories. Text classification can be used to guide the content and tone of the text generated by an AI language model, depending on the desired category or genre of the text.

Language generation: This involves using NLP models and algorithms to generate natural language output that is relevant and appropriate for a given task. Language generation techniques can be used to generate text based on the input provided in a prompt, taking into account the desired task, context, and constraints.

In conclusion, NLP plays a crucial role in AI prompt engineering by enabling the development of effective prompts that guide an AI language model to generate relevant and appropriate text for a given task. By leveraging NLP techniques such as text preprocessing, sentiment analysis, named entity recognition, text classification, and language generation, AI prompt engineers can design prompts that effectively communicate the task, context, and desired output to the AI language model.

Understanding of key NLP concepts such as tokenization, lemmatization, and part-of-speech tagging

Tokenization, lemmatization, and part-of-speech tagging are all key concepts in natural language processing (NLP) that are used to process and analyze text data.

Tokenization is the process of breaking down a piece of text into individual units, or tokens, such as words, phrases, or sentences. Tokenization is often the first step in NLP tasks, as it allows for more granular analysis of text data. For example, consider the following sentence: "The quick brown fox jumped over the lazy dog." The tokenization of this sentence would result in the following tokens: ["The", "quick", "brown", "fox", "jumped", "over", "the", "lazy", "dog", "."]

Lemmatization is the process of reducing words to their base or dictionary form, or lemma. This can help to standardize variations of a word and reduce the dimensionality of text data. For example, the word "running" can be reduced to its lemma "run". Similarly, the words "am", "is", and "are" can all be reduced to the lemma "be". Lemmatization can be performed using NLP tools such as NLTK or spaCy.

Part-of-speech (POS) tagging is the process of identifying the grammatical components of a sentence and labeling them with their corresponding part of speech, such as noun, verb, adjective, or adverb. POS tagging can be used to extract information about the syntax and structure of a sentence, which can be useful for many NLP tasks. For example, consider the following sentence: "The cat sat on the mat." A POS tagger would identify the parts of speech as follows: "The/DT cat/NN sat/VBD on/IN the/DT mat/NN."

In practice, these NLP concepts are often used together in NLP pipelines to process and analyze text data. For example, a typical NLP pipeline might involve tokenizing a piece of text, lemmatizing the tokens to their base forms, and then performing POS tagging to identify the parts of speech. This can then be used to extract information about the text, such as the main subjects and verbs, which can be used in downstream NLP tasks such as information retrieval or sentiment analysis.

Techniques for generating and refining prompts using NLP

Natural language processing (NLP) techniques can be used to generate and refine prompts by analyzing and manipulating text data. Here are some techniques for generating and refining prompts using NLP:

Text summarization: NLP techniques such as summarization can be used to generate concise summaries of longer pieces of text, which can be used as prompts for further analysis. For example, a long article about a company's financial results could be summarized into a few key points that can be used as prompts for further analysis.

Sentiment analysis: Sentiment analysis is a technique that uses NLP to identify and classify the emotional tone of a piece of text as positive, negative, or neutral. This can be useful for generating prompts that focus on specific emotions or sentiments, such as "Write a poem about love" or "Describe a time when you felt frustrated."

Named entity recognition: Named entity recognition is a technique that uses NLP to identify and extract named entities such as people, organizations, and locations from text data. This can be useful for generating prompts that focus on specific topics or themes, such as "Write a story about a famous scientist" or "Describe a trip to a foreign country."

Part-of-speech tagging: Part-of-speech tagging is a technique that uses NLP to identify and label the parts of speech in a piece of text. This can be useful for generating prompts that focus on specific types of words or sentence structures, such as "Write a sentence using a verb in the past tense" or "Write a haiku using only nouns and adjectives."

Language modeling: Language modeling is a technique that uses NLP to generate new text based on a given prompt or input. This can be useful for generating creative writing prompts or for generating variations on existing prompts. For example, a language model could be trained on a dataset of writing prompts and used to generate new prompts that are similar in theme or structure.

In practice, these techniques can be combined and iteratively refined to generate more specific and targeted prompts. For example, a prompt generator might use named entity recognition to identify a specific topic or theme, sentiment analysis to identify a desired emotional tone, and language modeling to generate a variety of possible prompts based on these criteria.

Chapter 4: Creating Effective AI Prompts

Guidelines for writing clear and concise prompts

Writing clear and concise prompts is essential for effective communication and successful completion of tasks. Here are some guidelines for writing clear and concise prompts:

Be specific: The prompt should be specific and clearly state what needs to be done. Avoid vague or ambiguous language that could be interpreted in multiple ways. For example, instead of saying "Write a story," say "Write a story about a person overcoming a challenge."

Use active voice: Use active voice to make the prompt more engaging and to clearly identify who is responsible for completing the task. For example, instead of saying "A story should be written," say "Write a story."

Keep it simple: Use simple and straightforward language that is easy to understand. Avoid using jargon or technical terms that may be unfamiliar to the reader. Use short and concise sentences to convey the message.

Avoid unnecessary words: Remove any unnecessary words or phrases that do not add value to the prompt. For example, instead of saying "In order to complete the task," say "To complete the task."

Provide context: Provide enough context for the prompt to be easily understood. This includes information about the audience, purpose, and desired outcome. For example, instead of saying "Write a poem," say "Write a love poem for Valentine's Day."

Be positive: Use positive language to create a positive tone and encourage the reader to complete the task. For example, instead of saying "Do not use passive voice," say "Use active voice to make your writing more engaging."

Test the prompt: Test the prompt with a small group of people to ensure that it is clear and concise. Ask for feedback on how the prompt could be improved.

Exercise:

Here's an example of a prompt that could be improved:

Poor prompt: "The objective of this task is to design and develop a software program. The software program should be user-friendly and efficient. The user should be able to navigate through the different features easily. The software program should also be secure and reliable."

Improved prompt: "Design and develop a user-friendly and efficient software program that allows users to easily navigate through its features. Ensure that the program is secure and reliable."

How to incorporate context and user intent into prompts

Incorporating context and user intent into prompts can help ensure that the task is completed successfully and efficiently. Here are some ways to do so:

Identify the audience: Consider who will be completing the task and what their needs and goals are. This will help ensure that the prompt is tailored to their specific context and user intent.

Provide background information: Provide any necessary background information to give the user context about why the task is important and what they are expected to accomplish. This could include information about the project, organization, or industry.

Use examples: Use examples to illustrate what is expected of the user and how the task should be completed. This can help the user understand the context and user intent of the prompt.

Ask questions: Ask questions to help the user clarify their understanding of the task and their goals. This can help ensure that the prompt is tailored to their specific context and user intent.

Use language that reflects the user's goals: Use language that reflects the user's goals and intentions. For example, if the user's goal is to increase sales, use language that emphasizes the importance of increasing sales in the prompt.

Consider the user's experience level: Consider the user's experience level when designing the prompt. If the user is a beginner, provide more context and guidance to help them understand the task. If the user is experienced, provide less guidance and more freedom to complete the task in their own way.

Provide feedback: Provide feedback on the user's progress and completion of the task. This can help the user understand the context and user intent of the prompt and make adjustments as needed.

Exercise:

Here's an example of a prompt that incorporates context and user intent:

Prompt: "As a marketing professional, your goal is to create a social media campaign that targets a younger demographic for our new line of skincare products. Use language and visuals that appeal to this demographic and highlight the unique benefits of our products. Consider using influencer partnerships to increase engagement. Your campaign should be launched within the next two weeks."

In this prompt, the context is clearly identified as marketing and the user intent is to create a social media campaign that targets a younger demographic for a specific product line. The prompt provides guidance on how to achieve this goal by suggesting the use of language, visuals, and influencer partnerships. The timeframe for completion is also provided to ensure that the user understands the urgency of the task.

The role of creativity in prompt engineering

Creativity plays an important role in prompt engineering as it allows for the development of prompts that are engaging, thought-provoking, and effective in achieving their intended purpose. Here are some ways that creativity can be used in prompt engineering:

Using creative language: Using creative language can help make prompts more engaging and memorable. This can include the use of metaphors, similes, alliteration, and other literary devices to capture the user's attention and help them remember the task.

Developing unique scenarios: Developing unique scenarios can help make prompts more interesting and relevant to the user's experience. This can include creating hypothetical situations or drawing from real-life experiences to make the task more relatable.

Incorporating humor: Incorporating humor can help make prompts more engaging and enjoyable to complete. This can include using puns, jokes, or other forms of humor to make the task more enjoyable and less tedious.

Encouraging creativity from users: Encouraging users to be creative in completing the task can help make the prompt more engaging and increase user satisfaction. This can include providing opportunities for users to personalize the task or express their creativity in completing the task.

Using visual elements: Using visual elements such as images, videos, or info graphics can help make prompts more engaging and visually appealing. This can help capture the user's attention and make the task more memorable.

Exercise:

Here's an example of a prompt that incorporates creativity:

Prompt: "Imagine you are a travel blogger with a passion for food. Your mission is to create a guide to the best street food in Bangkok. Your guide should include mouth-watering photos, insider tips, and your personal favorite dishes. Surprise us with your creativity and make us want to book a ticket to Thailand today!"

In this prompt, the user is given a scenario that allows for creativity in creating a guide to the best street food in Bangkok. The prompt encourages the user to use their passion and personal experience to create a guide that is engaging and memorable. The use of language such as "surprise us" and "make us want to book a ticket" encourages the user to think outside the box and create a guide that is unique and compelling. Overall, the prompt leverages creativity to create a task that is both interesting and effective in achieving its intended purpose.

Tips and tricks for creating effective AI prompts

Creating effective AI prompts can be a challenging task, but there are several tips and tricks that can help ensure success. Here are some tips and tricks for creating effective AI prompts:

Keep it simple: Use simple and concise language in your prompts. Avoid using technical jargon or complex sentence structures that may confuse the user.

Be clear: Make sure your prompts are clear and easy to understand. Avoid using ambiguous language or vague instructions that may lead to confusion.

Provide context: Provide enough context so that the user understands the purpose of the prompt and how it fits into the larger task. This can include providing background information or explaining the desired outcome.

Use examples: Use examples to help clarify the task and provide a clear understanding of what is expected. This can include providing sample responses or demonstrating how to complete the task.

Use visual aids: Use visual aids such as images, videos, or infographics to help clarify the task and provide context. This can help the user better understand the task and make it more engaging.

Test and iterate: Test your prompts with a small group of users to gather feedback and make improvements. Use this feedback to iterate on the prompts and make them more effective.

Consider user experience: Consider the user experience when designing prompts. Make sure the prompts are engaging and enjoyable to complete.

Exercise:

Here's an example of an effective AI prompt:

Prompt: "Write a short paragraph describing your favorite childhood memory. Be sure to include sensory details such as sights, sounds, and smells."

This prompt is simple, clear, and provides context for the user. It uses sensory details to help the user focus on the key elements of the task and encourages them to be descriptive in their response. The prompt also uses an engaging and relatable topic (childhood memories) to make the task more enjoyable to complete.

Best practices for refining prompts

Refining prompts is an important part of the AI prompt engineering process, and there are several best practices to follow to ensure that prompts are effective and produce accurate results. Here are some best practices for refining prompts:

Collect feedback: Collect feedback from users and stakeholders to identify areas of the prompt that may be confusing or unclear. This feedback can help you make improvements to the prompt and ensure that it is effective.

Evaluate performance: Evaluate the performance of the prompt by analyzing the responses generated by the AI model. Look for patterns or common errors in the responses that may indicate problems with the prompt.

Use data analysis tools: Use data analysis tools to analyze the responses generated by the AI model. This can help you identify areas of the prompt that may need to be refined.

Refine language: Refine the language of the prompt to make it more clear and concise. Avoid using technical jargon or complex sentence structures that may be confusing to users.

Provide context: Provide context for the prompt to help users understand the purpose of the task and how it fits into the larger workflow.

Iterate: Iterate on the prompt by making small changes and testing the results. This can help you identify areas of the prompt that may need further refinement.

Test with real data: Test the prompt with real data to ensure that it is effective in producing accurate results.

Exercise:

Here's an example of a prompt that has been refined using best practices:

Initial prompt: "Write a paragraph about your favorite food."

Refined prompt: "Write a paragraph about your favorite food, including the specific ingredients and flavors that make it unique. Consider using descriptive language to help the reader understand why this food is your favorite."

The refined prompt provides more context for the user and encourages them to be more descriptive in their response. The prompt also provides specific guidance on what to include in the response, which can help ensure that the AI model produces accurate results. By iterating on the prompt and making small changes, the refined prompt is more effective in achieving the desired outcome.

Common mistakes to avoid when creating prompts

When creating prompts, it's important to avoid common mistakes that can lead to confusion or misunderstanding among the audience. Here are some common mistakes to avoid:

Vague or ambiguous language: When creating a prompt, make sure to use clear and concise language that leaves no room for interpretation. Avoid using vague or ambiguous words that can be interpreted in different ways. For example, instead of saying "Write about a happy experience," say "Describe a time when you felt the happiest."

Exercise: Rewrite the following vague prompt to make it more specific and clear:
"Write about a memorable moment."

Asking multiple questions: Avoid asking multiple questions in one prompt, as this can confuse the audience and make it difficult for them to focus on one particular topic. Instead, focus on one specific question or topic. For example, instead of saying "What are your hobbies and interests? How do you spend your free time?", say "What is your favorite hobby, and how did you become interested in it?"

Exercise: Rewrite the following prompt to focus on one specific topic:
"Describe your favorite book and the author's writing style."

Using complicated language or concepts: Keep in mind that not everyone in your audience may be familiar with certain concepts or technical terms. Avoid using complicated language or concepts that may be difficult for some people to understand. Instead, use simple and clear language that is easy to understand. For example, instead of saying "Discuss the implications of quantum mechanics on modern physics," say "Explain how quantum mechanics has influenced modern physics."

Exercise: Rewrite the following prompt using simple and clear language:
"Examine the role of epigenetic in the development of cancer."

Being too broad or too narrow: Avoid creating prompts that are too broad or too narrow. A prompt that is too broad may be overwhelming for the audience, while a prompt that is too narrow may limit their creativity and ability to explore different ideas. Instead, aim for a prompt that is specific and focused, but also allows for some flexibility and creativity. For example, instead of saying "Write about your life," say "Describe a turning point in your life that changed your perspective."

Exercise: Rewrite the following prompt to make it more focused and specific:
"Write about a historical event."
By avoiding these common mistakes, you can create prompts that are clear, engaging, and effective in encouraging creativity and critical thinking.

5: Implementing AI Prompts in Your Writing

Techniques for integrating AI prompts into your writing

Integrating AI prompts into your writing can be a great way to enhance your creativity and explore new ideas. Here are some techniques you can use to integrate AI prompts into your writing:

Use AI-generated prompts as inspiration: You can use AI-generated prompts as a starting point for your writing, using them as inspiration to explore new ideas and topics. For example, an AI-generated prompt might be "Write a story about a character who can time travel," which could inspire you to explore themes like fate, destiny, and the consequences of our actions.

Exercise: Use an AI-generated prompt and write a short story that explores the themes suggested by the prompt.

Combine AI-generated prompts with your own ideas: You can also combine AI-generated prompts with your own ideas to create something truly unique. For example, you might combine an AI-generated prompt like "Write a story about a robot who learns to love" with your own idea of setting the story in a post-apocalyptic world, creating a unique story that combines themes of love and survival.

Exercise: Combine an AI-generated prompt with your own idea to create a short story that explores a unique theme.

Use AI to generate prompts tailored to your interests: You can also use AI to generate prompts that are tailored to your specific interests and preferences. For example, if you're interested in science fiction, you can use an AI-powered writing tool to generate prompts that are specifically geared towards that genre.

Exercise: Use an AI-powered writing tool to generate prompts tailored to your interests, and choose one to write a short story about.

By integrating AI prompts into your writing, you can open up new avenues for creativity and explore new ideas and themes. Whether you use them as inspiration or as a starting point for your own ideas, AI prompts can be a powerful tool for writers of all levels.

Best practices for integrating AI prompts into different types of writing

Integrating AI prompts into different types of writing can be done using best practices that are specific to each type of writing. Here are some best practices for integrating AI prompts into different types of writing:

Fiction writing: When using AI prompts in fiction writing, it's important to use them as a starting point rather than relying solely on them to guide your story. AI prompts can provide inspiration and help you explore new ideas, but they should not dictate the direction of your story. For example, if an AI prompt suggests a plot twist that doesn't fit with the rest of your story, it's okay to deviate from the prompt.

Let's say you're writing a science fiction story and you're stuck on how to introduce a new character. You could use an AI prompt such as "Create a character who has been frozen in cryo sleep for 100 years." You could then use this prompt as a starting point to create a new character, exploring their motivations and desires. For example, you could create a character who wakes up in a future world that's vastly different from the one they knew, and who must come to terms with their new reality.

Exercise: Use an AI prompt to create a character, and then write a short story that explores their motivations and desires.

Academic writing: When using AI prompts in academic writing, it's important to ensure that the prompt aligns with the research question or topic being studied. The prompt should be used as a tool to generate ideas and explore different angles of the topic. It's also important to ensure that any information or data generated by AI is credible and reliable.

Let's say you're writing a research paper on the impact of social media on mental health. You could use an AI tool to generate prompts related to this topic, such as "Examine the impact of social media on self-esteem," or "Analyze the relationship between social media use and anxiety." You could then use these prompts to explore different angles of the topic, using research and data to support your arguments.

Exercise: Use an AI tool to generate prompts related to your research question or topic, and use them to explore different angles of the topic.

Creative writing: When using AI prompts in creative writing, it's important to embrace experimentation and playfulness. AI prompts can provide unexpected combinations of words or concepts that can inspire creativity and help you generate new ideas. It's also important to not limit yourself to the prompt, but to explore different directions and ideas that may come up during the writing process.

Let's say you're interested in writing poetry and you're looking for inspiration. You could use an AI tool to generate a series of prompts related to a specific theme, such as "Write a poem about the ocean at sunset," or "Create a poem about the changing seasons." You could then use these prompts as inspiration to write a series of poems that explore different aspects of the theme.

Exercise: Use an AI tool to generate a series of prompts related to a specific theme or topic, and use them as inspiration to create a series of poems or short stories.

In all of these examples, the AI prompts are used as a starting point or a tool to generate ideas and inspiration. It's important to not limit yourself to the prompt, but to explore different directions and ideas that may come up during the writing process. By embracing experimentation and playfulness, you can use AI prompts to enhance your creativity and explore new ideas and perspectives.

By following these best practices, you can integrate AI prompts into different types of writing in a way that enhances your creativity and helps you explore new ideas and perspectives.

Strategies for working with AI language models that have limited capacity or accuracy

Working with AI language models that have limited capacity or accuracy can be challenging, but there are strategies you can use to make the most of these models. Here are some strategies for working with AI language models that have limited capacity or accuracy:

Simplify your prompts: When working with a limited AI language model, it's important to keep your prompts simple and concise. Avoid using complex language or sentence structures that the model may struggle with.

For example, instead of asking the AI to "Generate a detailed description of a medieval castle," you could simplify the prompt to "Describe a castle."

Example prompt: "Describe the human brain in detail."

Exercise: Try simplifying a prompt related to a topic you're interested in and see how the AI responds.

Use context: AI language models can struggle with generating text that is coherent and relevant to the topic at hand. To help the model better understand the context of your prompt, provide additional information or context. For example, instead of simply asking the AI to "Write a story about a dog," you could provide more context by saying "Write a story about a dog who gets lost in the woods."

Example prompt: "Write a story about a girl who discovers a mysterious object in her backyard and sets out on an adventure to uncover its secrets."

Exercise: Practice providing additional context for a prompt and see how it affects the quality of the AI's response.

> **Edit and refine:** Even with limited capacity or accuracy, AI language models can still provide useful insights and ideas. However, it's important to edit and refine the output to ensure that it meets your needs. This may involve rephrasing sentences, removing irrelevant information, or adding your own voice to the text.

Example output from AI language model: "Are you searching for the perfect gift for your friend? Look no further! Our online store has a wide selection of gifts that are sure to please anyone."

Example edited and refined text: "Looking for the perfect gift for your friend? Our online store offers a wide selection of unique and thoughtful gifts that are sure to make their day. Browse our collection today!"

By using these strategies, you can work effectively with AI language models that have limited capacity or accuracy, and still generate useful content and ideas.

Exercise: Take a text generated by an AI language model with limited capacity or accuracy and edit it to improve its quality.

By using these strategies, you can make the most of AI language models with limited capacity or accuracy, and still generate useful insights and ideas.

Examples of how AI prompts can be used in different types of writing (e.g., blogs, articles, social media posts)

AI prompts can be used in various types of writing to generate new ideas, add unique perspectives, or simply save time. Here are some examples of how AI prompts can be used in different types of writing:

> **Blogging:** Bloggers can use AI prompts to generate topic ideas, titles, or even outlines for their blog posts. For example, a blogger who writes about healthy living might use an AI prompt to generate a list of potential topics,

such as "10 Healthy Snacks to Boost Your Energy."

Let's say you run a blog on cooking and want to generate topic ideas for your next post. You could use an AI prompt to generate a list of potential topics, such as "10 Creative Recipes Using Leftover Vegetables" or "Healthy Snacks for Kids: 15 Simple and Delicious Ideas."

Example AI prompt: "Generate a list of potential topics for a cooking blog."

Exercise: Try using an AI prompt to generate a potential topic for your next blog post.

Articles: Writers who produce articles for online or print publications can use AI prompts to generate ideas or angles for their articles. For example, a journalist covering a breaking news story might use an AI prompt to generate a unique angle or perspective on the story.

Let's say you are a journalist covering a major news story, such as the COVID-19 pandemic. You could

use an AI prompt to generate a unique angle or perspective on the story, such as "How the Pandemic Has Changed the Way We Work: Insights from Experts."
Example AI prompt: "Generate a unique angle or perspective on the COVID-19 pandemic."

Exercise: Try using an AI prompt to generate a unique angle or perspective on a news story or current event.

> **Social media posts:** Social media managers can use AI prompts to generate catchy headlines or engaging captions for their posts. For example, a social media manager for a fashion brand might use an AI prompt to generate a catchy caption for an Instagram post showcasing a new clothing line.

Let's say you are a social media manager for a beauty brand and want to generate a catchy headline for an Instagram post showcasing a new product. You could use an AI prompt to generate a potential headline, such as "Get Glowing Skin with Our New Radiance-Boosting Serum."

Example AI prompt: "Generate a catchy headline for an Instagram post showcasing a new beauty product."

By using AI prompts in these ways, writers can generate new ideas, angles, or perspectives that they may not have thought of on their own. They can also save time and create more engaging and interesting content that resonates with their audience.

Exercise: Try using an AI prompt to generate a catchy headline or caption for a social media post.
In each of these examples, AI prompts are used to generate new ideas or perspectives, save time, or add a unique element to the writing. By using AI prompts in this way, writers can enhance their writing and create more engaging and interesting content.

Ethical considerations when using AI prompts for content creation

When using AI prompts for content creation, there are several ethical considerations to keep in mind. Here are some examples:

> **Bias:** AI prompts are only as unbiased as the data they are trained on. If the training data is biased, the prompts generated by the AI may also be biased. It's important to be aware of any biases in the data and take steps to address them.

Example: If you are using an AI prompt to generate content about gender, be aware that the training data may reflect gender bias. Take steps to ensure that the content you create is inclusive and does not perpetuate gender stereotypes.

> **Plagiarism:** AI prompts can be a helpful tool for generating ideas and inspiration, but it's important to avoid copying content directly from the prompts. Plagiarism is unethical and can result in legal consequences.

Example: If an AI prompt suggests a sentence or phrase that you like, rephrase it in your own words or use it as inspiration for your own original content.

Transparency: If you are using AI prompts to generate content, it's important to be transparent about it. Disclose that you are using AI prompts to your audience to avoid misleading them.

Example: If you are a blogger and are using AI prompts to generate content, mention it in the post or in a disclaimer on your blog.

Exercise: Think of a scenario where you might use an AI prompt to generate content. What ethical considerations should you keep in mind? How can you address these considerations in your content creation process?

By being mindful of ethical considerations when using AI prompts for content creation, writers can create content that is unbiased, original, and transparent. This not only ensures ethical standards are met, but also helps build trust with the audience.

6: Advanced AI Prompt Engineering Techniques

Advanced techniques for creating and refining AI prompts

Creating and refining AI prompts can be a challenging task, but there are several advanced techniques that can help improve the quality of prompts and the performance of AI models. Here are some techniques and exercises that young beginners can try:

Use OpenAI's GPT-3 language model: GPT-3 is one of the most advanced language models available, and it can generate high-quality prompts with minimal human intervention. Young beginners can try using GPT-3 to generate prompts for a variety of tasks, such as text completion, summarization, and translation.

Use transfer learning: Transfer learning is a technique that involves pre-training a model on a large dataset and then fine-tuning it for a specific task. Young beginners can try using transfer learning to create prompts for a variety of tasks, such as sentiment analysis, image recognition, and speech recognition.

Use active learning: Active learning is a technique that involves selecting a small subset of the data to train the model and then iteratively selecting more data points to train the model. Young beginners can try using active learning to create prompts for a variety of tasks, such as document classification, text clustering, and recommendation systems.

Use reinforcement learning: Reinforcement learning is a technique that involves training a model to take actions that maximize a reward signal. Young beginners can try using reinforcement learning to create prompts for a variety of tasks, such as game playing, robotics, and natural language processing.

Some examples of how the advanced techniques mentioned earlier can be applied to different tasks:

Text completion using GPT-3:

Prompt: "The quick brown fox jumps over the"
Output: "lazy dog. The fox's swift movements were a sight to behold as it gracefully leapt over the dog."

Summarization using transfer learning:

Prompt: "Summarize the article 'The Rise of Artificial Intelligence' in 100 words."
Output: "The article 'The Rise of Artificial Intelligence' discusses the increasing prevalence of AI in various industries and the potential benefits and drawbacks of this trend. The author argues that while AI has the potential to revolutionize many aspects of our lives, it also raises ethical and social concerns that must be addressed."

Translation using active learning:

Prompt: "Translate the phrase 'Hello, how are you?' from English to Spanish."
Output: "Hola, ¿cómo estás?" (Note: The model would require training on a bilingual dataset to perform accurate translations.)

Sentiment analysis using reinforcement learning:

Prompt: "Analyze the sentiment of the following text: 'I loved the movie I watched last night.'"
Output: "Positive." (Note: The model would be trained to recognize positive, negative, and neutral sentiment based on a labeled dataset.)

Image recognition using transfer learning:

Prompt: "Identify the object in the following image."
Output: "A dog." (Note: The model would be pre-trained on a large dataset of images and fine-tuned on a specific object recognition task.)

Speech recognition using active learning:

Prompt: "Transcribe the following audio clip into text."
Output: "I'm sorry, I didn't catch that." (Note: The model would require training on a dataset of audio clips and corresponding transcriptions to accurately transcribe speech.)

Exercise:

As a beginner exercise, young readers can try generating prompts using GPT-3 for a variety of tasks, such as:

Text completion: Given a sentence or phrase, generate a complete paragraph.

Summarization: Given a long article or document, generate a summary.

Translation: Given a sentence or phrase in one language, generate a translation in another language.

Sentiment analysis: Given a text, determine the sentiment (positive, negative, or neutral).

Image recognition: Given an image, identify the object or objects in the image.

Speech recognition: Given an audio clip, transcribe the speech into text.

By practicing these exercises, young beginners can gain experience in creating and refining AI prompts using advanced techniques.

Strategies for optimizing AI prompts for specific purposes (e.g., marketing, SEO)

Optimizing AI prompts for specific purposes, such as marketing or SEO, requires a different set of strategies than optimizing prompts for general use. Here are some strategies and exercises that young beginners can try:

Use specific keywords and phrases: When optimizing prompts for SEO or marketing, it's important to include specific keywords and phrases that are relevant to the topic or product. For example, if you're creating prompts for a marketing campaign for a new coffee shop, you might include keywords like "coffee", "latte", and "cappuccino".

Focus on user intent: When optimizing prompts for marketing or SEO, it's important to focus on the user's intent and create prompts that are relevant to their needs. For example, if you're creating prompts for a health and fitness website, you might create prompts that address common user questions or concerns, such as "How to lose weight in a healthy way" or "The benefits of strength training for women".

Use persuasive language: When optimizing prompts for marketing, it's important to use persuasive language that encourages the user to take action. For example, you might create prompts that use phrases like "limited time offer" or "exclusive deal" to encourage users to make a purchase or sign up for a service.

Some examples of how to optimize AI prompts for specific purposes:

SEO optimization:

Prompt: "What are some healthy recipes for weight loss?"

Optimization: "Discover delicious and nutritious weight loss recipes with these top healthy ingredients: low-fat dairy, lean protein, whole grains, and fresh fruits and veggies. Try our tasty low-calorie breakfast, lunch, and dinner ideas today!"

In this example, the prompt includes specific keywords ("healthy recipes" and "weight loss") and uses language that is optimized for search engines.

Marketing optimization:

Prompt: "Why choose our running shoes?"

Optimization: "Get the most out of your workouts with our high-performance running shoes. Designed with cutting-edge technology and premium materials, our shoes offer superior comfort, support, and durability. Plus, with a 100% satisfaction guarantee, you can feel confident in your purchase." In this example, the prompt addresses the user's intent by highlighting the features and benefits of the product, and uses persuasive language to encourage the user to make a purchase.

Persuasive language:

Prompt: "Sign up for our newsletter and get 10% off your next purchase!"
Optimization: "Don't miss out on exclusive deals, insider tips, and the latest news from our brand. Sign up for our newsletter today and get 10% off your next purchase! Plus, you'll be the first to know about new products and special promotions."
In this example, the prompt uses persuasive language ("exclusive deals", "insider tips", "latest news") to encourage the user to sign up for the newsletter, and offers a discount as an incentive.

By optimizing AI prompts for specific purposes, such as SEO or marketing, you can increase their effectiveness and achieve your desired outcomes.

Exercise:

As a beginner exercise, young readers can try optimizing prompts for specific purposes using the strategies mentioned above. For example:

SEO optimization: Given a topic like "healthy eating", create prompts that include specific keywords and phrases that are relevant to the topic, such as "nutrition", "healthy recipes", and "superfoods".

Marketing optimization: Given a product like "running shoes", create prompts that focus on the user's intent and address common questions or concerns related to the product, such as "How to choose the right running shoes for your feet" or "The benefits of wearing proper running shoes".

Persuasive language: Given a product like "vacation packages", create prompts that use persuasive language to encourage users to make a purchase, such as "Book now and save 50%" or "Don't miss out on this exclusive offer".

By practicing these exercises, young beginners can gain experience in creating AI prompts that are optimized for specific purposes and designed to achieve specific goals, such as improving search engine rankings or increasing sales.

Techniques for fine-tuning AI language models for specific purposes (e.g., sentiment analysis, summarization)

Fine-tuning AI language models for specific purposes requires a different set of techniques than creating and optimizing prompts. Here are some strategies and exercises that young beginners can try:

Collect and prepare training data: To fine-tune an AI language model, you need a large and diverse set of training data that is relevant to the specific task or purpose. For example, if you're fine-tuning a model for sentiment analysis, you might collect a dataset of customer reviews and ratings.

Choose a pre-trained language model: There are many pre-trained language models available, such as GPT-3 and BERT, that you can use as a starting point for fine-tuning. Choose a model that is suited to the specific task or purpose, and has been pre-trained on a large and diverse set of data.

Fine-tune the model: Once you have your training data and pre-trained model, you can fine-tune the model using techniques like transfer learning and hyperparameter tuning. This involves training the model on your specific dataset and adjusting the model's parameters to optimize its performance for the specific task or purpose.

Example of how to fine-tune an AI language model for sentiment analysis:

Collect and prepare training data: Let's say you want to analyze customer sentiment for a restaurant. You might collect a dataset of customer reviews from Yelp or Google Reviews, and label each review as positive, negative, or neutral based on the overall sentiment.

Choose a pre-trained language model: For sentiment analysis, you might choose a pre-trained language model like BERT, which has been pre-trained on a large corpus of text data.

Fine-tune the model: To fine-tune BERT for sentiment analysis, you would train the model on your specific dataset of customer reviews, adjusting the model's parameters to optimize its performance for the sentiment classification task. You might also use techniques like transfer learning and hyper parameter tuning to improve the model's accuracy.

Once the model is fine-tuned, you can use it to analyze new customer reviews and classify the sentiment as positive, negative, or neutral. For example, given the following customer review:
"Great food and friendly service, but the wait times are too long."

The fine-tuned BERT model might classify the sentiment as neutral, based on the mixed sentiment in the review.

By fine-tuning AI language models for specific purposes like sentiment analysis, summarization, and translation, you can create powerful tools that can automate tasks and save time and effort.

Exercise:

As a beginner exercise, young readers can try fine-tuning an AI language model for a specific purpose using the strategies mentioned above. For example:

Sentiment analysis: Given a dataset of customer reviews for a product or service, fine-tune a pre-trained language model like BERT to accurately classify the sentiment of each review as positive, negative, or neutral.

Summarization: Given a set of long-form articles or documents, fine-tune a pre-trained language model like GPT-3 to generate accurate and concise summaries of the text.

Translation: Given a set of documents in one language, fine-tune a pre-trained language model like Google Translate to accurately translate the text into another language.

By practicing these exercises, young beginners can gain experience in fine-tuning AI language models for specific purposes and improve their skills in natural language processing.

Tips for improving the accuracy and fluency of generated text

Improving the accuracy and fluency of generated text is a crucial aspect of natural language processing. Here are some tips and exercises that young beginners can try to improve the quality of generated text:

Increase training data: The quality of generated text can be improved by increasing the amount and diversity of training data. This can include adding more examples of relevant text or using data augmentation techniques to generate new examples.

Fine-tune model hyperparameters: Model hyperparameters such as learning rate, batch size, and optimizer can have a significant impact on the quality of generated text. Experimenting with different hyperparameter settings can help to identify the optimal combination for a specific task or purpose.

Control generation: Controlling the generation process can improve the accuracy and fluency of the generated text. Techniques like temperature scaling, nucleus sampling, and top-p sampling can help to control the randomness of the generated text.

Some examples of how to improve the accuracy and fluency of generated text:

Increase training data: Let's say you want to generate product descriptions for an online store. You might increase the amount and diversity of training data by scraping product descriptions from other online stores, or by using data augmentation techniques like replacing synonyms or paraphrasing existing descriptions.

Fine-tune model hyperparameters: To improve the accuracy and fluency of generated text, you might experiment with different hyperparameter settings. For example, you might try using a larger batch size or a smaller learning rate to improve the quality of the generated text. Alternatively, you might try using a different optimizer like Adam or RMSprop to see if it produces better results.

Control generation: To improve the accuracy and fluency of the generated text, you might use techniques like temperature scaling, nucleus sampling, or top-p sampling. For example, you might use temperature scaling to control the randomness of the generated text, or use nucleus sampling to generate text with a higher probability of generating coherent sentences.

Overall, by practicing these techniques and experimenting with different settings and approaches, you can improve the quality of generated text and develop your skills in natural language processing.

Exercise:

To improve the accuracy and fluency of generated text, young beginners can try the following exercise:

Fine-tune a pre-trained language model: Start by fine-tuning a pre-trained language model like GPT-3 or BERT for a specific task, such as generating product descriptions or summarizing news articles.

Experiment with hyperparameters: Try adjusting the model hyperparameters to see how they impact the quality of the generated text. For example, you could experiment with different learning rates or batch sizes to see which settings produce the most accurate and fluent text.

Control generation: Use techniques like temperature scaling, nucleus sampling, and top-p sampling to control the generation process and improve the accuracy and fluency of the generated text.

By practicing these exercises, young beginners can gain experience in improving the accuracy and fluency of generated text and develop their skills in natural language processing.

Approaches for handling out-of-domain prompts and unfamiliar topics

Handling out-of-domain prompts and unfamiliar topics is a common challenge in natural language processing. Here are some approaches and exercises that young beginners can try to handle these issues:

Data augmentation: Data augmentation techniques can be used to increase the diversity of the training data and make the model more robust to out-of-domain prompts and unfamiliar topics. For example, you might use paraphrasing or back-translation to generate new training examples that cover a wider range of topics and domains.

Fine-tuning on related tasks: Fine-tuning the language model on related tasks can improve its ability to handle out-of-domain prompts and unfamiliar topics. For example, if you are building a chatbot for customer support, you might fine-tune the model on a dataset of customer support tickets to make it more familiar with the domain-specific language and topics.

Zero-shot learning: Zero-shot learning is a technique where the model is trained to generate text for a set of tasks, even if it has never seen those tasks before. This can be useful for handling unfamiliar topics and out-of-domain prompts. For example, if you train a language model on a diverse set of tasks like summarization, translation, and question answering, it may be able to generate text for a new task without any additional training.

some examples of how to handle out-of-domain prompts and unfamiliar topics:

Data Augmentation: Let's say you are training a language model to generate product descriptions for an online store. To handle out-of-domain prompts and unfamiliar topics, you might use data augmentation techniques like paraphrasing or back-translation. For example, you might paraphrase existing product descriptions to create new training examples, or back-translate descriptions from another language to increase the diversity of the training data.

Fine-tuning on related tasks: Let's say you are building a chatbot to provide customer support for an online store. To handle out-of-domain prompts and unfamiliar topics, you might fine-tune the language model on a dataset of customer support tickets. This would help the model become more familiar with the domain-specific language and topics that customers might ask about.

Zero-shot learning: Let's say you have trained a language model on a diverse set of tasks, including summarization, translation, and question answering. To handle an unfamiliar topic or out-of-domain prompt, you might use zero-shot learning to generate text for a new task without any additional training. For example, you could prompt the model with a question about a topic it has never seen before, and it may be able to generate a coherent response based on its understanding of language and reasoning.

Overall, these approaches can help young beginners develop their skills in handling out-of-domain prompts and unfamiliar topics, and build more robust and versatile language models.

Exercise:

To practice handling out-of-domain prompts and unfamiliar topics, young beginners can try the following exercise:

a)Train a language model on a specific domain or topic, such as sports news or scientific research.

b)Use data augmentation techniques to generate new training examples that cover a wider range of topics and domains.

c)Fine-tune the model on related tasks, such as summarization or question answering, to improve its ability to handle out-of-domain prompts.

d)Test the model on a set of prompts that are outside its training domain or topic, and evaluate its performance.

By practicing these exercises, young beginners can develop their skills in handling out-of-domain prompts and unfamiliar topics, and build more robust and versatile language models.

Chapter 7: Challenges and Limitations of AI Prompt Engineering

Ethical considerations when using AI prompts

There are several ethical considerations to keep in mind when using AI prompts, especially given the challenges and limitations of AI prompt engineering. Here are some key points to consider, along with examples and exercises for young beginners:

Bias and fairness: AI prompt engineering can perpetuate biases and inequalities if the data used to train the models is biased or incomplete. For example, if a language model is trained on a dataset that includes only data from a particular group or culture, it may generate biased or offensive text when prompted with data from other groups or cultures. Young beginners should be aware of the potential for bias and take steps to ensure that their training data is diverse and representative.

Exercise: Collect a dataset of text from a variety of sources, and analyze it for potential biases or stereotypes. Use techniques like counterfactual analysis or adversarial training to mitigate these biases and improve the fairness of your language model.

Privacy and consent: AI prompt engineering can involve collecting and using personal data, which raises privacy and consent concerns. For example, if a language model is trained on private conversations or sensitive information, it may violate the privacy of the individuals involved. Young beginners should be mindful of these privacy concerns and take steps to ensure that their use of personal data is transparent and ethical.

Exercise: Develop a privacy policy and consent form for collecting and using data for your language model. Ensure that the policy and form are clear and transparent, and provide users with options for opting out or deleting their data.

Responsibility and accountability: AI prompt engineering can have real-world consequences, and it is important to consider the potential impacts of the generated text. For example, if a language model is used to generate fake news or propaganda, it may contribute to social and political unrest. Young beginners should be aware of their responsibility and accountability when using AI prompts, and take steps to ensure that their text generation is ethical and responsible.

Exercise: Develop a code of ethics for using AI prompts, and identify potential risks and harms associated with the generated text. Consider the potential impact on different groups of people, and develop guidelines for mitigating these risks and harms.

By considering these ethical considerations and engaging in exercises like the ones outlined above, young beginners can develop their skills in ethical and responsible AI prompt engineering.

Legal and ethical implications of using AI-generated content in different contexts

The use of AI-generated content can have legal and ethical implications in various contexts. Here are some key points to consider, along with examples and exercises for young beginners:

Intellectual property: AI-generated content can raise intellectual property issues if it is created using copyrighted material or if it infringes on the rights of other creators. For example, if a language model generates text that is similar to an existing book or article, it may infringe on the copyright of the original author. Young beginners should be aware of these intellectual property issues and take steps to ensure that their use of AI-generated content is legal and ethical.

Exercise: Research copyright laws and fair use guidelines in your country, and apply them to your use of AI-generated content. Identify potential infringement risks and develop strategies for avoiding them.

Misinformation: AI-generated content can contribute to the spread of misinformation and fake news, which can have significant social and political consequences. For example, if a language model generates text that is misleading or inaccurate, it may contribute to public confusion or distrust. Young beginners should be aware of these risks and take steps to ensure that their use of AI-generated content is ethical and responsible.

Exercise: Develop a fact-checking system for verifying the accuracy of AI-generated content. Use techniques like source verification and cross-checking to ensure that the generated text is reliable and trustworthy.

Bias and discrimination: AI-generated content can perpetuate biases and inequalities if it is trained on biased or incomplete data. For example, if a language model generates text that is offensive or discriminatory, it may contribute to social or cultural harm. Young beginners should be aware of these risks and take steps to ensure that their use of AI-generated content is fair and inclusive.

Exercise: Conduct a bias audit of your training data and language model, and identify potential sources of bias or discrimination. Use techniques like counterfactual analysis or adversarial training to mitigate these biases and improve the fairness of your language model.

By considering these legal and ethical implications and engaging in exercises like the ones outlined above, young beginners can develop their skills in responsible and ethical use of AI-generated content.

Limitations of current AI technology and potential pitfalls to avoid

While AI technology has made tremendous progress in recent years, it still has some limitations and potential pitfalls to avoid. Here are some key points to consider, along with examples and exercises for young beginners:

Bias and limitations of training data: AI models are only as good as the data they are trained on. If the training data is biased or incomplete, the model may not generalize well to new situations or populations. For example, if a language model is trained on text from a particular demographic group, it may not perform well on text from other groups. Young beginners should be aware of these limitations and take steps to ensure that their training data is diverse and representative.

Exercise: Collect and label a diverse set of text data for training a language model, and evaluate the performance of the model on different subgroups of the data.

Lack of transparency and interpretability: Many AI models are "black boxes," meaning that it can be difficult to understand how they arrive at their decisions or generate their output. This lack of transparency can make it difficult to diagnose and correct errors or biases. Young beginners should be aware of these limitations and take steps to ensure that their models are transparent and explainable.

Exercise: Use techniques like explainable AI or model interpretation to understand how your language model generates its output, and identify potential sources of error or bias.

Overfitting and generalization: AI models can sometimes be too good at fitting to the training data, leading to poor performance on new or unseen data. This is known as overfitting. Conversely, models can also underfit or fail to capture important patterns in the data. Young beginners should be aware of these pitfalls and take steps to ensure that their models are properly trained and validated.

Exercise: Use techniques like cross-validation or hyperparameter tuning to optimize the performance of your language model on new or unseen data.

By considering these limitations and potential pitfalls and engaging in exercises like the ones outlined above, young beginners can develop their skills in responsible and effective use of AI technology.

Strategies for overcoming common challenges in AI prompt engineering

There are several common challenges in AI prompt engineering, but there are also strategies for overcoming them. Here are some key points to consider, along with examples and exercises for young beginners:

Lack of training data: AI models require large amounts of data to learn patterns and generate output. If there is a lack of training data, the model may not perform well. One strategy for overcoming this challenge is to use transfer learning, which involves using a pre-trained model as a starting point and fine-tuning it on a smaller set of domain-specific data.

Exercise: Use transfer learning to fine-tune a pre-trained language model on a smaller set of domain-specific data, and compare its performance to a model trained from scratch.

Difficulty in creating high-quality prompts: Creating high-quality prompts is crucial for generating accurate and fluent output from AI models. However, it can be difficult to create prompts that are specific and clear enough to guide the model. One strategy for overcoming this challenge is to use template-based prompts, which provide a structured format for input and guide the user to provide the necessary information.

Exercise: Create a set of template-based prompts for a language model, and evaluate their effectiveness in generating accurate and fluent output.

Lack of diversity in training data: AI models can be biased if the training data is not diverse enough. This can lead to inaccurate or unfair output. One strategy for overcoming this challenge is to use data augmentation, which involves creating new training examples by modifying or combining existing ones.

Exercise: Use data augmentation techniques like paraphrasing or back-translation to increase the diversity of training data for a language model, and evaluate the impact on the model's accuracy and fairness.

By considering these strategies and engaging in exercises like the ones outlined above, young beginners can develop their skills in effective AI prompt engineering.

Here are some examples to illustrate the strategies for overcoming common challenges in AI prompt engineering:

Lack of training data: Let's say you want to build a language model to generate product descriptions for a new line of clothing. However, you only have a small dataset of a few hundred product descriptions to work with. To overcome this challenge, you could use a pre-trained language model like GPT-2 as a starting point, and fine-tune it on your small dataset using transfer learning.

Difficulty in creating high-quality prompts: Let's say you want to build a chatbot that can answer customer questions about a new software product. However, it can be difficult to create prompts that are specific and clear enough to guide the chatbot. To overcome this challenge, you could use template-based prompts like "What is the purpose of the software?" or "How do I install the software?" to guide the user and ensure that the chatbot has the necessary information to provide a helpful response.

Lack of diversity in training data: Let's say you want to build a sentiment analysis model to classify customer reviews of a new restaurant. However, your training data is limited to reviews from a single demographic group, and you're concerned about the potential for bias. To overcome this challenge, you could use data augmentation techniques like paraphrasing or back-translation to create new training examples and increase the diversity of the data. This can help ensure that the model is able to accurately classify reviews from a wider range of customers.

Future directions for AI prompt engineering

Future directions for AI prompt engineering include:

a) Developing more advanced and efficient techniques for generating high-quality prompts, such as using reinforcement learning to optimize the prompts over time.

b) Integrating human feedback and expertise into the prompt engineering process to improve the quality and accuracy of the models.

c) Exploring new use cases for AI prompt engineering, such as using prompts to generate creative content like music or art.

d) Improving the interpretability and explain ability of AI models to better understand how prompts are impacting the output.

e) Continuing to develop more diverse and representative training data to reduce bias in AI models and ensure fairness and inclusivity.

An exercise for readers could be to explore one of these future directions and come up with a hypothetical scenario or use case where it could be applied. For example, a reader might explore the use of prompts to generate personalized workout plans for individuals, and consider how reinforcement learning could be used to optimize the prompts over time based on user feedback.

Chapter 8: Conclusion and Next Steps

Recap of key takeaways from the book

Chapter 1: AI Prompt Engineering is the process of designing prompts that can be used to generate text using AI language models. It is important to learn AI Prompt Engineering because it has many real-world applications, such as content creation, customer service, and chatbots.

Chapter 2: AI language models are the heart of AI Prompt Engineering. They use machine learning algorithms to predict the most probable next word in a given sentence. Choosing the right language model for your needs is crucial.

Chapter 3: A prompt is a sentence or phrase that provides context for the AI language model to generate text. A good prompt should be clear, concise, and relevant to the task at hand. NLP plays a significant role in prompt engineering, and techniques such as tokenization, lemmatization, and part-of-speech tagging can be used to generate and refine prompts.

Chapter 4: Writing effective AI prompts requires creativity and attention to detail. Guidelines for clear and concise prompts include incorporating context and user intent and avoiding common mistakes.

Chapter 5: Integrating AI prompts into your writing requires careful consideration of the type of content being created. Best practices for integrating AI prompts and strategies for working with AI language models with limited capacity or accuracy should be considered.

Chapter 6: Advanced AI prompt engineering techniques include optimizing prompts for specific purposes such as marketing and SEO, fine-tuning language models for sentiment analysis and summarization, and improving accuracy and fluency of generated text. Approaches for handling out-of-domain prompts and unfamiliar topics should also be considered.

Chapter 7: Ethical considerations when using AI prompts include legal and ethical implications of using AI-generated content and potential pitfalls to avoid. Strategies for overcoming common challenges in AI prompt engineering and future directions for AI prompt engineering are also discussed.

Overall, AI Prompt Engineering has numerous practical applications, and with careful consideration of ethical implications and best practices, it has the potential to greatly benefit many industries.

Resources for further learning and practice

There are many resources available for further learning and practice in AI prompt engineering. Some of these include:

Online courses: There are several online courses available that cover various aspects of AI prompt engineering. Some popular platforms that offer these courses include Coursera, Udacity, and edX.

Books: There are many books available that cover different aspects of AI and natural language processing. Some popular titles include "Deep Learning" by Ian Goodfellow, Yoshua Bengio, and Aaron Courville, and "Natural Language Processing with Python" by Steven Bird, Ewan Klein, and Edward Loper.

Online communities: There are many online communities where you can connect with other AI enthusiasts and practitioners. Some popular communities include Reddit's /r/artificial and /r/MachineLearning, and the AI section of Stack Exchange.

Practice platforms: There are several online platforms where you can practice creating AI prompts and working with language models. Some popular platforms include Hugging Face's Transformers and OpenAI's GPT-3 Playground.

Conferences and workshops: Attending conferences and workshops is a great way to stay up-to-date with the latest advancements in AI and to network with other professionals in the field. Some popular conferences and workshops include the Neural Information Processing Systems (NeurIPS) conference and the Association for Computational Linguistics (ACL) conference.

Exercise: Choose one of the above resources and spend some time exploring it. Take notes on what you learn and consider how you can apply this knowledge to your own AI prompt engineering projects.

Examples of innovative uses of AI prompts in different industries

AI prompts have numerous innovative uses in various industries, some of which are:

A)Healthcare: AI prompts can be used to prompt patients to take their medication on time. AI-powered virtual assistants can provide reminders to patients through SMS or voice messages.

B)Education: AI prompts can be used to assist students in their learning by providing feedback and guidance. Teachers can create prompts that help students learn concepts better or ask them to write an essay on a topic and then analyze their responses using AI tools.

C)Marketing: AI prompts can be used to create personalized marketing campaigns. For instance, prompts can be designed to gather information about a customer's preferences and then use that data to create targeted advertisements.

D)Journalism: AI prompts can be used to assist journalists in their writing. Journalists can use prompts to quickly generate article summaries or provide suggested headlines for their stories.

E)Customer service: AI prompts can be used to create chat bots that help customers find answers to their queries. Chat bots can be programmed to understand customer requests and respond appropriately, thereby improving the customer experience.

Examples of innovative uses of AI prompts include:

The use of AI-powered chat bots in the banking industry to help customers with their financial needs.

Example:
Prompt: "What can I help you with today? You can ask me questions about your account balance, recent transactions, or even get personalized investment advice."

The use of AI prompts in the legal industry to help lawyers draft contracts and analyze legal documents.

Example:
Prompt: "Please provide me with the relevant information, and I'll generate a draft contract for you. This includes the parties involved, the terms of the agreement, and any additional requirements or clauses you would like to include."

The use of AI prompts in the entertainment industry to generate scripts for movies and TV shows.

Examples:

Prompt: "Please provide me with some details about your project, such as the genre, characters, and plot. Based on that, I'll generate a script for you."

The use of AI prompts in the automotive industry to generate design ideas and improve vehicle safety.

Example:
Prompt: "Please provide me with some design specifications, such as desired features, color scheme, and any safety requirements. Based on that, I'll generate some design ideas for you to consider."

The use of AI prompts in the gaming industry to create personalized gaming experiences.

Example:

Prompt: "What kind of gaming experience are you looking for? I can generate personalized game scenarios and characters based on your preferences and playstyle."

Exercise:

Think of an industry or field that interests you and come up with an innovative use of AI prompts in that field. Write a brief explanation of how AI prompts could be used and what benefits it could offer.

Final thoughts on the importance of AI prompt engineering

AI prompt engineering plays a crucial role in enabling effective communication between humans and machines. By creating prompts that can be understood and acted upon by AI language models, we can leverage the power of these models to enhance a wide range of industries and applications. Through understanding the fundamentals of prompt engineering, choosing the right AI language model, creating effective prompts, implementing them in writing, and using advanced techniques, we can unlock the full potential of AI technology. However, it is important to keep in mind the ethical considerations and limitations of AI technology and to continuously learn and improve our prompt engineering practices. Overall, AI prompt engineering is a valuable skill that can lead to more efficient and innovative ways of using AI technology to meet our needs and solve real-world problems.

Final thoughts on the importance of AI prompt engineering

AI prompt engineering is a crucial component in the development of effective and efficient natural language processing systems. As the demand for AI-generated content continues to increase, it is becoming increasingly important to ensure that the prompts used to generate this content are of high quality and free from biases. The use of AI prompts has a wide range of real-world applications, from customer service chatbots to content creation in the entertainment industry. Therefore, understanding and mastering the fundamentals of AI prompt engineering can provide individuals and organizations with a competitive advantage. By implementing the strategies and techniques discussed in this field, individuals can generate more accurate and fluent text, optimize AI models for specific purposes, and avoid common pitfalls and ethical concerns. Overall, the importance of AI prompt engineering cannot be understated, and it will continue to play a critical role in the development and deployment of AI language models in the future.

The importance of ongoing learning and experimentation in AI prompt engineering

AI prompt engineering is a rapidly evolving field, with new models, techniques, and best practices emerging all the time. As such, it's essential for practitioners to engage in ongoing learning and experimentation to stay up-to-date with the latest developments and to continue improving their skills.

Continual learning can involve attending conferences, workshops, and online courses, as well as reading industry blogs, articles, and research papers. It's also crucial to experiment with new approaches and techniques, as this can help practitioners discover new ways of generating effective prompts and refining AI language models.

By embracing ongoing learning and experimentation, practitioners can remain at the forefront of the field and continue to produce high-quality; effective AI prompts that meet the needs of their clients and users.

Future directions for AI prompt engineering and the role of beginners in shaping the field.

In the future, AI prompt engineering is expected to become more sophisticated and more accessible to non-experts. As the field continues to evolve, beginners will play an important role in shaping its development. By exploring new approaches to prompt engineering and experimenting with different techniques, beginners can help to drive innovation and progress in the field. As AI becomes increasingly integrated into our daily lives, the ability to create effective prompts will become an essential skill for writers, marketers, and other content creators. Therefore, ongoing learning and experimentation are critical for staying up-to-date with the latest developments in AI prompt engineering and continuing to improve our ability to generate high-quality content using AI technology.

9. Career options for AI Prompt Engineer

Job options for AI Prompt Engineer

As an AI Prompt Engineer, there are several career options that you can pursue. Here are some examples:

Natural Language Processing (NLP) Engineer: As an NLP Engineer, you will be responsible for designing and developing algorithms and models to analyze and understand natural language text and speech data.

Machine Learning Engineer: As a Machine Learning Engineer, you will be responsible for designing and building machine learning models to enable intelligent decision making and automation.

Data Scientist: As a Data Scientist, you will work on analyzing and interpreting complex data using statistical and machine learning techniques. You will help organizations make data-driven decisions.

AI Researcher: As an AI researcher, you will conduct research on AI algorithms and develop new techniques to improve AI models.

Robotics Engineer: As a Robotics Engineer, you will design, develop, and maintain robotic systems that use AI algorithms to perform various tasks.

AI Product Manager: As an AI Product Manager, you will be responsible for developing and managing AI-based products, defining product strategy, and working with engineering teams to implement and launch new features.

AI Ethics and Policy Advisor: As an AI Ethics and Policy Advisor, you will work with organizations to develop ethical guidelines for AI development and deployment, as well as advise on AI-related policy issues.

These are just a few examples of career options for an AI Prompt Engineer. The field of AI is growing rapidly, and new opportunities are emerging all the time.

Freelancing and business options for AI Prompt Engineer

As an AI Prompt Engineer, there are several freelancing and business options that you can pursue. Here are some examples:

Freelancing as an AI consultant: As an AI consultant, you can offer your expertise to businesses or individuals who are looking to implement AI solutions in their projects. You can provide advice on the best AI tools and techniques to use, as well as help with the development and deployment of AI models.

Offering AI training and coaching services: You can also offer training and coaching services to individuals or businesses that are looking to learn more about AI. This could include teaching programming languages such as Python and R, as well as teaching machine learning and deep learning techniques.

Developing and selling AI-based products: You can develop AI-based products such as chatbots, recommendation engines, and predictive analytics tools, and sell them to businesses or individuals. This could be done through online marketplaces such as Amazon or Etsy.

Building custom AI solutions for businesses: You can work with businesses to build custom AI solutions tailored to their specific needs. This could involve designing and developing AI models, as well as providing ongoing support and maintenance.

Creating and selling AI-based courses and tutorials: You can create and sell online courses and tutorials on AI topics such as machine learning, deep learning, and natural language processing.

Starting an AI consulting firm: You can start your own consulting firm focused on AI solutions. This could involve building a team of AI experts and offering services such as AI strategy consulting, AI model development, and AI implementation services.

These are just a few examples of freelancing and business options for an AI Prompt Engineer. With the growing demand for AI solutions, there are many opportunities for AI experts to build successful careers as freelancers or business owners.

www.ingramcontent.com/pod-product-compliance
Lightning Source LLC
Chambersburg PA
CBHW072240150726
48002CB00005B/2173